FAST AND FURIOUS
MONSTER TRUCKS
AND OTHER BEASTS OF THE ROAD

Clive Gifford

Ticktock

An Hachette UK Company

www.hachette.co.uk

First published in Great Britain in 2014 by Ticktock,
an imprint of Octopus Publishing Group Ltd
Endeavour House
189 Shaftesbury Avenue
London
WC2H 8JY

www.octopusbooks.co.uk

www.ticktockbooks.co.uk

ISBN 978 1 78325 138 4

A CIP record for this book is available from the British Library.

Printed and bound in China

1 3 5 7 9 10 8 6 4 2

Design: Freeland Design

Publisher: Samantha Sweeney Managing Editor: Karen Rigden
Production Controller: Sarah Connelly

CONTENTS

**MEET THE BEASTS
OF THE ROAD**   4

MONSTER TRUCKS   6
Afterburner   8
Avenger   10
Backwards Bob   12
Bad Habit   14
Batman   16
Bear Foot   18
Bigfoot   20
Bigfoot 17   22
Boogey Van   24
Bounty Hunter   26
Captain Crusher   28
Grave Digger   30
Jurassic Attack   32
Shell Camino   34
Snake Bite   36
Swamp Thing   38
War Wizard   40

WORK TRUCKS   42
BelAZ 75710   44
Cat 797F   46
Liebherr T282B   48
Mack Titan   50
AA-60 tank truck   52
Big Wind   54

Colet K/40E Jaguar   56
Oshkosh P-15 ARFF   58
Dodge Power Wagon model   60
International CXT   62
Gibbs Humdinga   64
Hurricane tractor   66
Liebherr LTM 11200-9.1   68

BIG RACING TRUCKS   70
Banks Freightliner
Pikes Peak Racer   72
British Pickup Truck Racer   74
Chevrolet Silverado
NASCAR Truck   76
Kamaz 4326
Dakar Rally Truck   78
MAN TGS Race Truck   80
Renault-MKR
Technology Race Truck   82
Shockwave   84
Tata Prima Race
Truck 4038.S   86
Toyota Tundra
NASCAR Truck   88
V8 Ute Racing Series   90

RECORD BREAKERS   92

GLOSSARY   94

MEET THE BEASTS OF THE ROAD

Every day millions of trucks are at work, on and off road, as they haul heavy loads, race to fight fires or entertain people at shows, races and events. This book showcases some of the most stunning, spectacular and famous trucks ever to wow crowds and thrill fans at races.

MONSTER TRUCKS

Marvel at the pioneering Bigfoot and Bear Foot monster trucks and how they helped create a whole new style of racing and entertainment. Check out record-breaking vehicles like Bad Habit, Monster Jam favourites like Grave Digger and Bounty Hunter and learn more about how these trucks are built and prepared to race not just in North America but all over the world.

TRUCKS AT WORK

Discover some of the biggest, baddest trucks ever built for work and tough tasks. Wonder at the world's biggest dump truck, the BelAZ 75710, giant fire tenders, hefty production pickups like the International CXT as well as the Gibbs Humdinga (below), an ingenious truck equally at home on land or water.

RACING TRUCKS

Find out about big racing rigs such as the MAN TGS (below), desert-racing trucks from Tata and Kamaz and the power-packed trucks of NASCAR like the Chevrolet Silverado.

MONSTER TRUCKS

Monster trucks are built to race, perform stunts and entertain. These mean machines have powerful engines, giant wheels and super-sized suspension systems which enable them to race hard over dirt courses, leap off ramps and pull off stunts.

MONSTER TRUCKS RULE!

Monster trucks that take part in major competitions have to follow rules. Trucks must weigh at least 4 tonnes (9,000lb) and have safety features such as kill switches which turn off power immediately if there's a problem.

MONSTER JAM

Monster truck racing started in America but has since spread all over the world. There are many different competitions, but the biggest is Monster Jam. Over four million fans watch Monster Jam events, which have been held in 40 different countries, and many millions more follow the action on TV or over the Internet.

This shows the size of man compared to a monster truck, in this case, Grave Digger.

AFTERBURNER

Afterburner is a monster truck champion. It won the 2009 Monster Jam World Finals Freestyle Championship. The truck scored 36 out of 40 points to beat 23 rivals in front of over 40,000 fans at the Sam Boyd Stadium in Las Vegas.

Afterburner's body came from a 2006 Cadillac Escalade SUV (sports utility vehicle).

Freestyle competitions see trucks spend 60 or 90 seconds tackling a course full of tough obstacles and jumps. The performance is judged by a panel of officials. Extra points may be awarded for trick moves such as pulling a wheelie.

DID YOU KNOW?

Toy company Mattel made model Afterburners 43 times smaller than the original.

STATS AND FACTS

FIRST BUILT: 2006

BUILDER: FELD ENTERTAINMENT

ORIGIN: US

MAXIMUM POWER: 1,465 BHP

FAMOUS DRIVERS: PAUL COHEN, DAMON BRADSHAW, COTY SAUCIER

ENGINE TYPE: MERLIN 540

ENGINE SIZE: 8.85 LITRES

FUEL: HIGH-OCTANE RACING METHANOL

WEIGHT: AROUND 4,536KG (10,000LB)

AVENGER

In 1957, Chevrolet made a car that would become an American classic, the Chevy Bel Air. Forty-five years later, a monster truck built from the body of a Bel Air took the Monster Jam by storm.

Avenger was first built in 1996 using a Chevy S-10 pickup truck as its base. It was remodelled in 2002. It won the World Freestyle Championship twice – in 2003 and 2011.

The distance between the middle of the front and back wheels is called a truck's wheelbase. Avenger's wheelbase is 3.5m (138in).

STATS AND FACTS

FIRST BUILT: 1997

BUILDER: AVENGER RACING

ORIGIN: US

MAXIMUM POWER: 1,850BHP

FAMOUS DRIVERS: JIM KOEHLER

ENGINE TYPE: BLOWN 575 CHEVROLET BIG BLOCK

ENGINE SIZE: 9.42 LITRES

FUEL: HIGH-OCTANE RACING METHANOL

WEIGHT: 4,309KG (9,500LB)

BACKWARDS BOB

In most monster trucks the driver sits facing forwards in the centre of the cab. Backwards Bob is different. Its body is mounted on the chassis the other way round so the driver looks out of the back of the cab over the rear of the truck.

Backwards Bob made its debut at the 2008 Monster Jam World Finals in Las Vegas. It never fails to impress: every time it appears, Backwards Bob thrills fans and even tricks people into believing that it's racing in reverse.

STATS AND FACTS

FIRST BUILT: 2008

BUILDER: UNKNOWN

ORIGIN: US

MAXIMUM POWER: 1,500BHP

FAMOUS DRIVERS: MIKE WINE, BARI MUSAWWIR, GEORGE BALHAN, DUSTIN BROWN

ENGINE TYPE: 540 CI MERLIN

ENGINE SIZE: 8.8 LITRES

FUEL: HIGH-OCTANE RACING METHANOL

WEIGHT: 4,535KG (10,000LB)

DID YOU KNOW?

Another back-to-front truck debuted at shows in America in 2012. Called WrongWay Rick, it features a Ford F-150 pickup truck body facing backwards and is driven by Rick Swanson.

The giant tyres are 1.68m (66in) high and 1.1m (43in) wide. They are known as Terra tyres and cost around £1,500 each.

BAD HABIT

The award for the longest jump is hotly competed for – meet the truck that just keeps winning!

In September 2013, Bad Habit, driven by Joe Sylvester, broke its own world record. It soared an incredible 72.39 metres (237ft 6in) into the air off a giant ramp, landing almost nose first.

Shock absorber tubes are filled with nitrogen gas. These help cushion the truck on landing by letting the wheels rise up to 66cm (26in) closer to the body.

A Cadillac Escalade formed the body of Bad Habit.

STATS AND FACTS

FIRST BUILT: 2008

BUILDER: JOE SYLVESTER AND JERRY RICHMOND

ORIGIN: US

MAXIMUM POWER: 1,400BHP

FAMOUS DRIVERS: JOE SYLVESTER

ENGINE TYPE: 540 CHEVROLET

ENGINE SIZE: 8.8 LITRES

FUEL: HIGH-OCTANE RACING METHANOL

WEIGHT: 4,627KG (10,200LB)

TRUCK STOP

Bad Habit beat its previous world record jump by 8.81 metres (28ft 10in)!

BATMAN

A hit with fans of superheroes and monster trucks, Batman is styled like the Batmobile from DC Comics and movies, complete with bat logos and three pretend jet engines sticking out the back.

DID YOU KNOW?

The driver of the crime-fighting Batman truck at the 2012 Monster Jam World Finals was a serving police officer, Norm Miller.

The jet engines might be fake but there's nothing fake about its performance. Batman has reached the Monster Jam World Finals four times and won the racing title twice.

STATS AND FACTS

FIRST BUILT: 2006

BUILDER: JAMIE DOWNS, TERRY PAYNE AND DOUG FORBES

ORIGIN: US

MAXIMUM POWER: 1,500BHP

Large sculpted fins form the fibreglass wings of the vehicle body.

FAMOUS DRIVERS: JOHN SEASOCK, JASON CHILDRESS, NORM MILLER

ENGINE TYPE: 540 MERLIN CHEVROLET

ENGINE SIZE: 8.8 LITRES

FUEL: HIGH-OCTANE RACING METHANOL

WEIGHT: APPROX. 4,535KG (10,000LB)

BEAR FOOT

After racing each other in dragsters in the 1970s, rivals Fred Shafer and Jack Willman Senior joined forces to make one of the first monster trucks. The original Bear Foot was built from a 1974 Chevrolet pickup and was one of the first rivals of Bigfoot (p20).

DID YOU KNOW?

Bear Foot started out on tyres 1.22m (48in) wide before becoming one of the first monster trucks to use the classic Terra tyres measuring 1.68m (66in) in width.

Bear Foot has been remodelled and updated an incredible 17 times during its long life. New Bear Foot trucks have also been built. In 1997, Bear Foot was sold to Paul Shafer (no relation to Fred!) who runs it in his team alongside Monster Patrol, Captain USA and other monster trucks.

STATS AND FACTS

FIRST BUILT: 1979 (ORIGINAL BEAR FOOT)

BUILDER: FRED SHAFER, JACK WILLMAN SR

ORIGIN: US

MAXIMUM POWER: 700BHP

FAMOUS DRIVERS: FRED SHAFER, PAUL SHAFER

ENGINE TYPE: 454 CHEVROLET

ENGINE SIZE: 7.4 LITRES

FUEL: PETROL

WEIGHT: APPROX. 8,165KG (18,000LB)

TRUCK STOP

Bear Foot got its name from Sugar and Spice, the two baby American black bears that Fred Shafer used to carry around when he took the truck to shows.

BIGFOOT

Bigfoot was the first monster truck ever built. Its owner used it to advertise his shop at car shows and tractor pulls. Then, in 1981, a video of the truck crushing two old cars suddenly made Bigfoot famous.

So many people wanted to see Bigfoot that its owner built another one. Today there are 20 different versions!

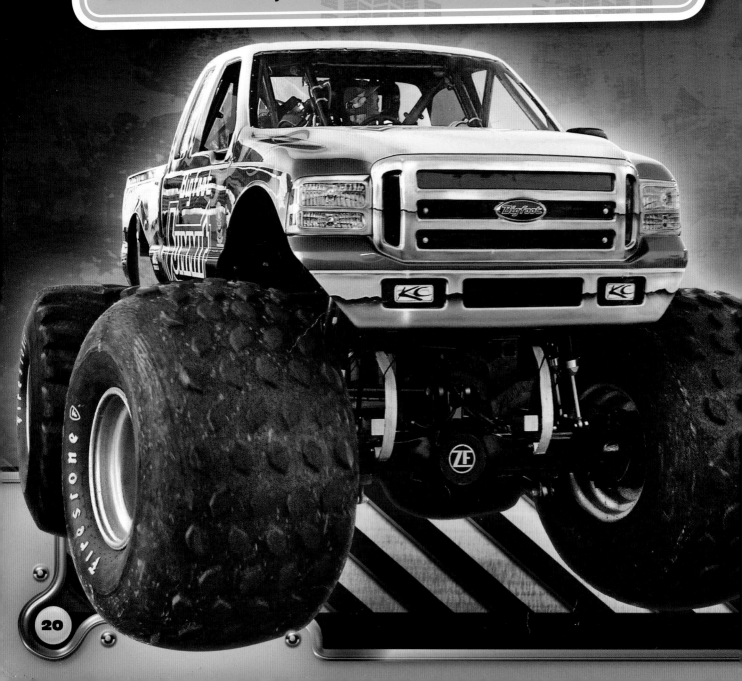

Bigfoot used strong axles from a military vehicle. These made it possible to fit huge tyres, and to steer using all four wheels.

STATS AND FACTS

FIRST BUILT: 1976

BUILDER: BOB CHANDLER

MAXIMUM POWER: 1,100 BHP (ABOUT TEN TIMES AS POWERFUL AS MOST HATCHBACKS)

FAMOUS DRIVERS: DAN RUNTE, RON BACHMAN, AMBER WALKER

ENGINE SIZE: 10.5 LITRES

ENGINE TYPE: 640 CI FORD

FUEL: HIGH-OCTANE RACING GASOLINE/NITROUS OXIDE

WEIGHT: 5,000KG (11,023LB)

BIGFOOT 17

Built in 2003, this was Europe's first Bigfoot truck. It was made by Nigel Morris with permission from Bob Chandler – creator of the original Bigfoot.

Bigfoot 17 has appeared not only in the UK but all over Europe and the Middle East. The truck also won four European Monster Truck Racing Championships (2003, 2006, 2007 and 2009).

Bigfoot 17's body is from a 1997 Ford F150 pickup truck. The truck took around seven months and £140,000 to build.

STATS AND FACTS

FIRST BUILT: 2003

BUILDER: NIGEL MORRIS

ORIGIN: UK/US

MAXIMUM POWER: 1,750BHP

FAMOUS DRIVERS: NIGEL MORRIS

ENGINE TYPE: 572 FORD RACING V8

ENGINE SIZE: 9.37 LITRES

FUEL: METHANOL

WEIGHT: 4,309KG (9,500LB)

TRUCK STOP

Bigfoot 17's giant engine uses up a lot of fuel – over 5 litres (1.3 gallons) for every 60 metres (197ft) travelled!

BOOGEY VAN

The Boogey Van was the first monster truck to be built using a van as a base vehicle. It took two years and around £60,000 to build Boogey Van, using a Ford Aerostar van for the body.

Massive shock absorbers allow the wheels to rise and fall up to 91cm (36in).

Pamela Vaters drove Boogey Van to become the first female driver in national monster truck competitions. In 1995, she finished 5th overall in the national points competition and she still holds the record for a female driver.

STATS AND FACTS

FIRST BUILT: 1993

BUILDER: MICHAEL VATERS

ORIGIN: US

MAXIMUM POWER: 1,500BHP

FAMOUS DRIVERS: PAMELA VATERS, MIKE BARNES, LINDSEY RETTEW

ENGINE TYPE: 572 C.I. FORD SVO ENGINE

ENGINE SIZE: 9.37 LITRES

FUEL: HIGH-OCTANE RACING METHANOL

WEIGHT: 4,685KG (10,328LB)

DID YOU KNOW?

A brand new Boogey Van came back with a bang in 2013, competing in the Monster X tour with a new female driver, Lindsey Rettew.

BOUNTY HUNTER

Jimmy Creten loved the monster trucks he saw at a 1995 show so much that he bought one himself. It would become known as Bounty Hunter and appear at 12 Monster Jam World Finals in a row (2002–13), winning the 2005 Freestyle competition.

Monster truck tyres such as those used on Bounty Hunter usually have 30–80kg (66–177lb) of rubber shaved off them by hand to save on weight, a job that can take up to 50 hours per tyre.

Bounty Hunter's original body came from a small Chevy S-10 pickup, but it was replaced in the mid-2000s with this new body from a Ford Explorer SUV.

STATS AND FACTS

FIRST BUILT: 1996

BUILDER: JIMMY CRETEN

ORIGIN: US

MAXIMUM POWER: 1,600BHP

FAMOUS DRIVERS: JIMMY CRETEN, DARREN MIGUES

ENGINE TYPE: 555 CI BLOWN

ENGINE SIZE: 9.09 LITRES

FUEL: HIGH-OCTANE RACING METHANOL

WEIGHT: 4,535KG (10,000LB)

TRUCK STOP

Jimmy often races against his wife, Dawn, who drives the Scarlet Bandit monster truck for the pair's 2XtremeRacing team.

CAPTAIN CRUSHER

Monster trucks draw big crowds in Australia and Captain Crusher was one of the most popular. It was part of a team of trucks raced by Clive Featherby, including Monster Patrol and Outback Thunda.

DAILY JUICE COMPANY

Captain Crush

We'll change anyth.

The truck's body is made from two different vehicles – a camper van and a cab from a 1998 Dodge Dakota Club pickup truck.

In 2006, Billy Featherby became the world's youngest monster truck driver, driving Captain Crusher at the age of 14 years and 18 days. His record didn't last long though – in 2008, his younger brother Jaye Featherby, driving Monster Patrol at a show in Toowoomba, Australia, beat the record by two days.

STATS AND FACTS

FIRST BUILT: 2005-06

BUILDER: CLIVE FEATHERBY/ KC'S FIREWORKS

ORIGIN: AUSTRALIA/US

MAXIMUM POWER: 1,700BHP

ENGINE TYPE: 580 CHEVROLET BIG BLOCK

FAMOUS DRIVERS: BILLY FEATHERBY, JAYE FEATHERBY, SHERRI SHAFFER

ENGINE SIZE: 9.37 LITRES

FUEL: HIGH-OCTANE RACING METHANOL

WEIGHT: 4,700KG (10,361LB)

GRAVE DIGGER

Dennis Anderson built his first monster truck in the 1980s using parts from a rusty 1950s Chevrolet pickup. There have been 29 Grave Diggers since then.

Grave Digger trucks proved both fast and spectacular freestyle performers, giving Dennis Anderson four Monster Jam world titles. Dennis's son, Adam, won both the 2013 and the 2014 World Racing Championship with the 29th Grave Digger, known as 'The Legend'. Some Grave Diggers are used as ride trucks to give fans a taste of the action but many still perform in arenas around the world.

This truck's body is made [of fi]breglass and [mo]delled on the [shape] of a 1950s [p]anel van.

STATS AND FACTS

FIRST BUILT: 1982

BUILDER: DENNIS ANDERSON

ORIGIN: US

MAXIMUM POWER: 1,500BHP

FAMOUS DRIVERS: DENNIS ANDERSON, CHARLIE PAUKEN, RANDY BROWN

ENGINE TYPE: 540 CHEVROLET BIG BLOCK

ENGINE SIZE: 8.85 LITRES

FUEL: HIGH-OCTANE RACING METHANOL

WEIGHT: 4,535KG (10,000LB)

TRUCK STOP

One of Grave Digger's trademarks is its red headlights, which create a dramatic contrast to its ghoulish black and green paint scheme.

JURASSIC ATTACK

Impressed with the body sculpting of Snake Bite (see p36), Don Frankish decided to design a new monster truck to look like a dinosaur. He first sketched out a T-Rex design, before deciding on a truck that looked like a Triceratops.

DID YOU KNOW?

A second Jurassic Attack truck has been built with extra seats to give rides to up to 10 passengers at a time.

Jurassic Attack has proven a big hit. It has travelled throughout Canada, the United States and Europe. In Wales, it won the 2007 Monster Jam Europe Freestyle Championship with a perfect score.

DID YOU KNOW?

The three Weenk brothers, Kevin, Linsey and Nathan, have all driven Jurassic Attack in competitions.

STATS AND FACTS

FIRST BUILT: 1999

BUILDER: DON FRANKISH AND LINSEY WEENK

ORIGIN: CANADA

MAXIMUM POWER: 1,500BHP

FAMOUS DRIVERS: DON FRANKISH, KEVIN WEENK, NATHAN WEENK, KRISTY EDGE AND GARY SCHOTT JR

ENGINE TYPE: 540 CHEVROLET

ENGINE SIZE: 8.8 LITRES

FUEL: HIGH-OCTANE RACING METHANOL

WEIGHT: 4,535KG (10,000LB)

SHELL CAMINO

Shelley Kujat wanted to prove that women are just as good as men when it comes to driving. For many years she drove a truck for a delivery company before taking up monster truck driving in 2000.

Shell Camino took Shelley and her husband 16 months to build. The truck features shock absorbers 66cm (26in) long, these make it strong enough to withstand all the bashes and high impact landings monster trucks experience in competition.

The tubular steel frame supports the fibreglass body, modelled on a 1972 Chevrolet El Camino SS.

TRUCK STOP

Another female monster truck driver, Debrah Miceli, won the 2005 Monster Jam World Finals, racing in her Madusa truck.

STATS AND FACTS

FIRST BUILT: 2006-07

BUILDER: SHELLEY AND RON KUJAT

ORIGIN: US

MAXIMUM POWER: 1,600BHP+

FAMOUS DRIVERS: SHELLEY KUJAT

ENGINE TYPE: 572 CHEVROLET BIG BLOCK

ENGINE SIZE: 9.37 LITRES

FUEL: HIGH-OCTANE RACING METHANOL

WEIGHT: 4,309KG (9,500LB)

SNAKE BITE

Snake Bite was built by the team behind the Bigfoot trucks. In fact, the first Snake Bite used Bigfoot 4's chassis and wheels. It was the first monster truck to feature a specially designed character body, shaped more like a snake's head than a truck.

Snake Bite's special body was moulded out of light but strong fibreglass, with bulges for the eyes of the snake's head and fangs over the front of the bonnet.

STATS AND FACTS

FIRST BUILT: 1991

BUILDER: BOB CHANDLER

ORIGIN: US

MAXIMUM POWER: 1,500BHP

FAMOUS DRIVERS: GENE PATTERSON, ERIC MEAGHER, DAN RUNTE

ENGINE TYPE: 572 FORD HEMI

ENGINE SIZE: 9.37 LITRES

FUEL: HIGH-OCTANE RACING METHANOL

WEIGHT: 4,535KG (10,000LB)

DID YOU KNOW?

The first driver of Snake Bite, Gene Patterson, called himself Colt Cobra and pretended to be from Cobra Creek, a place that doesn't exist. When racing he even wore a mask to hide his identity.

The snake design was added using an rush which uses pressed air to paint through a nozzle.

SWAMP THING

A truck with three different identities, Swamp Thing started out in America as Dragon Slayer and was then renamed Captain Insano. In 2000, the truck was shipped to the UK where Tony Dixon rebuilt it and named it after the Everglades swamps.

Swamp Thing came second in four European Monster Truck Racing Championships (2003, 2006, 2007 and 2009). It has also travelled back to America to take part in Monster Jam competitions.

TRUCK STOP

A remote-control model 10 times smaller than the real Swamp Thing went on sale in 2011. Powered by nitro gas, it can reach 56mph (90kph).

STATS AND FACTS

FIRST BUILT: 1994; RENAMED SWAMP THING IN 2002

BUILDER: KREG CHRISTENSEN

ORIGIN: US

MAXIMUM POWER: 1,450BHP

FAMOUS DRIVERS: TONY DIXON

ENGINE TYPE: 540 SUPERCHARGED TALL BLOCK

ENGINE SIZE: 8.85 LITRES

FUEL: METHANOL

WEIGHT: 5,000KG (11,023LB)

The 5.8m (19ft) long truck rides on eight large shock absorbers, each with 66cm (26in) of travel. The shock absorbers help the truck climb over wrecked cars with ease.

WAR WIZARD

With its sleek, streamlined body and incredibly powerful engine, War Wizard is one of the fastest monster trucks on the circuit. It can accelerate from zero to 60mph (96kph) in just 5.2 seconds – faster than many sports cars!

War Wizard can reach speeds of over 81mph (130kph) by burning the explosive methanol fuel used by most leading monster trucks. It uses around a litre of fuel for every 850m (2,788ft) it travels.

DID YOU KNOW?

It takes War Wizard around 59m (193ft) to brake from a speed of 70mph (112kph) and come to a standstill.

STATS AND FACTS

FIRST BUILT: 2008

BUILDER: RANDY MOORE

ORIGIN: US

MAXIMUM POWER: 1,810BHP

FAMOUS DRIVERS: RANDY MOORE

ENGINE TYPE: 572 FORD

ENGINE SIZE: 9.37 LITRES

FUEL: HIGH-OCTANE RACING METHANOL

WEIGHT: 4,535KG (10,000LB)

These are the stats and facts for the War Wizard 2 vehicle that Randy Moore has raced since 2008.

War Wizard was inspired by owner and driver Randy Moore's earlier career as a dragster racer. The fibreglass body is based on a 1941 Willys coupé car.

warwizardracing.com

WORK TRUCKS

Every day, millions of trucks go off to work. They vary greatly in size. The smallest are 3m-long mini-trucks powered by motorbike engines which carry small loads through narrow city streets. The largest are giant dump trucks transporting rock and earth at mines and large building sites.

LET'S GO TO WORK!

Check out these amazing work trucks including those that fight fires, haul massive loads and those that are incredibly versatile, like pickup trucks. Although small, pickup trucks can perform lots of jobs, from towing stranded cars to carrying hay in farm fields.

This shows the size of man compared to a huge dump truck, in this case a BelAZ 75710.

BELAZ 75710

Huge dump trunks are used in mining to remove large amounts of rock and soil from giant mines. None come bigger than the BelAZ 75710, which is the largest in the world and can carry up to 450 tonnes of rock.

The steel hopper can carry the same weight as 300 Ford Focus cars or 95 monster trucks.

The truck can withstand high and low temperatures of -50°C–50°C (-58°F–188°F). Its engines use around 1,300 litres (286 gallons) of fuel for every 62 miles (100km).

STATS AND FACTS

FIRST BUILT: 2013

ORIGIN: BELARUS

POWER: 2 X 2,300BHP

LENGTH: 20.6M (67FT 6IN)

WIDTH: 9.87M (32FT 4IN)

HEIGHT: 8.17M (26FT 9IN)

WEIGHT: UP TO 810,000KG (1,785,744LB) LOADED

FUEL: DIESEL

TRUCK STOP

Fully loaded, the BelAZ 75710 weighs more than an Airbus A380 airliner filled with over 800 passengers!

CAT® 797F

To get into the truck cab, which stands 5.2m (17ft) off the ground, drivers need to climb the large ladder running across the front of the truck's radiator.

This third-generation ultra-hauler dump truck from Caterpillar is strong enough to carry over 360 tonnes of rock and earth. Fully loaded, it can weigh over 600 tonnes.

All that weight needs a massive engine to move it. Where most monster truck engines are 7–10 litres in size, with a capacity of 106 litres the engine in the 797F is more than ten times bigger and gives the truck a top speed of 42mph (68 kph).

DID YOU KNOW?

A single tyre for a Cat 797F measuring 4m (13ft) high/wide weighs 5,300kg (11,685lb) and costs over £20,000 – more than many new cars.

STATS AND FACTS

FIRST BUILT: 2009

ORIGIN: US

POWER: 4,000BHP

LENGTH: 15.08M (49FT 6IN)

WIDTH: 9.75M (32FT)

HEIGHT: 7.7M (25FT 4IN)

WEIGHT: UP TO 623,690KG (1,375,001LB) LOADED

FUEL: DIESEL

LEIBHERR T282B

The T282B is an enormous hybrid dump truck. Hybrids use both diesel engines and electric motors to power the vehicle. The giant electric motors power the truck's rear wheels allowing T282B to reach a top speed of 40mph (64kph).

The massive hopper can carry up to 363 tonnes of rock and earth.

LIEBHERR

It takes just 22 seconds to empty its giant hopper: powerful hydraulic pistons push up the front of the hopper, tilting it so that the contents fall out of the back.

STATS AND FACTS

FIRST BUILT: 2004

ORIGIN: US

POWER: 3,650BHP

LENGTH: 15.32M (50FT 3IN)

WIDTH: 9.09M (29 FT 10IN)

HEIGHT: 7.84M (25FT 9IN)

WEIGHT: UP TO 592,000KG (1,305,136LB) LOADED

FUEL: DIESEL

TRUCK STOP

The Liebherr T282B is too big and heavy to travel on roads. It has to be shipped in crates from the factory and assembled over several weeks at its workplace.

MACK TITAN

John, Gus and William Mack built their first truck in 1907. Just over 100 years later, Mack Trucks introduced the Titan into North America. This big rig is designed for pulling extremely heavy loads over long distances.

The metal frame, called Bull Bars, protects the truck and driver in collisions.

Different types of trailers can be attached to the back of the Titan allowing it to haul big loads such as logs, giant bulldozers and other construction machines.

STATS AND FACTS

FIRST BUILT: 2008

ORIGIN: US

POWER: 605BHP

LENGTH: 7.95M (26FT 1IN)

HEIGHT: 3.01M (10FT 1IN) TO TOP OF CAB

WIDTH: 2.96M (9FT 9IN)

WEIGHT: UP TO 136,078KG (300,000LB) TRUCK AND TRAILER COMBINED WEIGHT

FUEL: DIESEL

DID YOU KNOW?

All Mack trucks carry a symbol of a bulldog, the nickname given to Mack trucks by soldiers who used them during the First World War for their strength and reliability.

AA-60 TANK TRUCK

The AA-60 was a fire engine used at airports and military airfields in the former Soviet Union, but it started out in the 1960s as a military weapon – a launcher for Scud missiles.

The truck's gigantic 38.8-litre engine (over four times the size of most monster truck engines) was originally designed for tanks. Despite its huge size, it only generated 525bhp, which is around a third of a typical monster truck.

The AA-60 was an 8x8 vehicle. This meant that power from the engine drove all eight wheels.

STATS AND FACTS

FIRST BUILT: 1983

ORIGIN: SOVIET UNION

POWER: 525BHP

LENGTH: 11.67M (38FT)

WIDTH: 3.07M (10FT)

HEIGHT: 2.92M (9FT 6IN)

WEIGHT: UP TO 44,850KG (98,877LB) LOADED

FUEL: DIESEL

TRUCK STOP

The original vehicle this fire engine was based on was known as Uragan, meaning 'hurricane' in Russian.

BIG WIND

Fires that start in oil wells can be extremely hard to put out as the oil is very flammable and fuels the fire. One ingenious truck uses jet engine power to literally blow the fire out with a massive blast of gas and water.

Big Wind (also known as Windy) is an old Russian T-34 tank from the Second World War. Mounted where its gun turret would be are two jet engines, which thrust out gases at high speed when switched on. Water is pumped into these gases, forming a powerful blast that wipes fires out.

The two Tumansky R-25 jet engines were originally used on MiG-21 jet fighter planes.

STATS AND FACTS

FIRST BUILT: 1991

ORIGIN: HUNGARY

POWER: 12,580BHP

LENGTH: 10.64M (34FT 10IN)

WIDTH: 4.34M (14FT 3IN)

HEIGHT: 3.98M (13FT 1IN)

WEIGHT: 41,730KG (91,998LB)

FUEL: DIESEL FOR THE TRUCK BODY, KEROSENE FOR THE JET ENGINES

DID YOU KNOW?

It's estimated that the truck's powerful pumps could suck up all the water in a swimming pool in less than a minute.

COLET K/ 40E JAGUAR

The giant boom can be raised over 13.4m (41ft) and shoot over 3,000 litres (793 gallons) of water per minute at a blaze.

The Colet K is a crash tender. These are specially built fire engines which operate mostly at airports and military airbases. They're designed to respond to fires and accidents fast and need to carry their fire-fighting chemicals and water with them.

The 8-wheeled vehicle is powered by two engines, one at the back and one at the front. It can accelerate from a standstill to 50mph (80kph) in 17 seconds, which is very fast for a large, heavy vehicle.

STATS AND FACTS

FIRST BUILT: 2009

ORIGIN: US

POWER: 1,000BHP (2 X 500BHP)

LENGTH: 12.1M (39FT 6IN)

WIDTH: 2.5M (8FT 6IN)

HEIGHT: 3.2M (10FT 8IN)

WEIGHT: UP TO 32,386KG (71,398LB) FULLY LOADED

FUEL: DIESEL

TRUCK STOP

K/15, K/40's little brother, is one of the fastest crash tenders around with a top speed of 83mph (133.5kph).

OSHKOSH P-15 ARFF

One of the biggest fire engines of all time, the P-15 Airport Rescue Fire Fighting (ARFF) truck could tackle big blazes affecting aircraft and airfields. Weighing more than 12 typical monster trucks, it needed two 495bhp engines to power its eight wheels.

Foam concentrate and 22,713 litres (6,000 gallons) of water could be stored inside the truck. When mixed together inside the truck, it could produce more than 227,000 litres (60,000 gallons) of foam to put fires out.

Powerful pumps enabled the truck to blast out up to 18,540 litres (4,900 gallons) of water and foam per minute.

TRUCK STOP

Tiny in comparison, the Polaris ATV 6x6 fire truck is just 3.6m (11ft 9in) long; powered by a 40bhp engine and carries 284 litres (75 gallons) of water. It's used to put out small brush fires in hard-to-reach places.

U.S. AIR FORCE

0460
105TH AW

STATS AND FACTS

FIRST BUILT: 1977

ORIGIN: US

POWER: 990BHP

LENGTH: 13.8M (45FT 2IN)

WIDTH: 3.1M (10FT)

HEIGHT: 4.2M (13FT 9IN)

WEIGHT: 59,000KG (130,860LB)

FUEL: DIESEL

DODGE POWER WAGON

The Dodge Power Wagon was a popular pickup truck from the 1950s onwards. Sheikh Hamad bin Hamdan Al Nahyan of the United Arab Emirates ordered a supersized version in 1994, much bigger than the original.

Each of the truck's wheels is 3m (9ft 10in) tall and comes from a giant vehicle that moved oil rigs.

The enormous truck is over 5m (16ft 4in) tall and has two floors inside which contain four bedrooms, a kitchen and a living room. The tailgate of the truck even opens out to form a large balcony.

STATS AND FACTS

FIRST BUILT: 1994

ORIGIN: UNITED ARAB EMIRATES

POWER: 300BHP (ENOUGH TO MOVE THE TRUCK SHORT DISTANCES)

LENGTH: APPROX. 19M (62FT 4 IN)

WIDTH: 8M (26FT 3IN)

HEIGHT: 5M (16FT 4IN)

WEIGHT: OVER 50 TONNES (50,000KG)

FUEL: DIESEL

DID YOU KNOW?

Sheikh Al Nahyan has a collection of over 300 other vehicles. Most are on display in a museum housed in a huge pyramid.

POWER WAGON

INTERNATIONAL CXT

The biggest production pickup truck in the world, the mighty CXT, was capable of carrying almost 6 tonnes (13,227lb) in its long pickup bed behind the cab. Its large 7.6-litre engine, almost the size of a monster truck engine, enabled the CXT to tow over 18 tonnes (39,681lb) in weight, such as a luxury yacht or horse trailer.

The six-wheeled CXT was produced between 2004 and 2008 along with two other models: a slimmer, smaller RXT and a heavily modified military truck, the MXT.

DID YOU KNOW?

The CXT was a big hit with celebrities. Basketball star Shaquille O'Neal and actor Ashton Kutcher are amongst many who bought one for a whopping £56,000–£67,000.

The large cab seats five people on air-sprung bucket seats to give a comfortable ride.

STATS AND FACTS

FIRST BUILT: 2004

ORIGIN: US

POWER: 220BHP

LENGTH: 6.6M (21FT 6IN)

WIDTH: 2.6M (8FT 5IN)

HEIGHT: 2.7M (9FT)

WEIGHT: UP TO 11,793KG (25,999LB) FULLY LOADED

FUEL: DIESEL

GIBBS HUMDINGA

Designed to reach really remote places, the Humdinga is equally at home on land and on water. Its supercharged V8 engine provides four-wheel drive on roads at speeds of 50mph (80kph) or more. To switch from land to water, all the driver has to do is press a button.

The 200-litre (53 gallon) fuel tank gives the Humdinga a combined range of 99 miles (160km) on land and a further 99 miles (160km) on water.

When entering water, the wheels rise up and tuck into the floating, waterproof body. The engine then powers jet thrusters which blast out water behind the Humdinga, pushing the vehicle through the water at up to 30mph (48kph).

STATS AND FACTS

FIRST BUILT: 2012

ORIGIN: NEW ZEALAND/US

POWER: 300BHP

LENGTH: 6.68M (21FT 9IN)

WIDTH: 2.09M (6FT 8 IN)

HEIGHT: 2.38M (7FT 9IN)

WEIGHT: 2,750KG (6,063LB)

FUEL: DIESEL OR PETROL VERSION

TRUCK STOP

Over a million hours of research and testing went into the design and building of the Humdinga and its sister truck, the Phibian.

HURRICANE TRACTOR

This is no ordinary tractor, Hurricane is a superstar in the world of tractor pulling where strong tractors running at maximum power compete to pull sleds weighing many tonnes along a straight course. Those that can haul the giant load the furthest win.

A small
l cage made
steel bars
otects the
ctor driver.

Hurricane competes in the Superstock class in the Netherlands and at the European Tractor Pulling Championships, but it began life as a Fendt 936 Vario farm tractor. It was modified to include four turbochargers and methyl alcohol fuel in order to boost the engine's power.

STATS AND FACTS

FIRST BUILT: 2006

ORIGIN: THE NETHERLANDS

POWER: 3,000BHP

LENGTH: 6M (19FT 8IN)

WIDTH: APPROX. 3.2M (10FT 5IN)

HEIGHT: APPROX. 2.4M (7FT 9IN)

WEIGHT: UNDER 3,500KG (7,716LB)

FUEL: METHYL ALCOHOL

TRUCK STOP

It took over 5,000 hours to build Hurricane and prepare it for competitive tractor pulling.

LIEBHERR LTM 11200-9.1

The world's biggest mobile telescopic crane, this 18-wheeler truck lifts heavy objects up high to help build skyscrapers, wind turbines and towers.

The crane part of the truck has its own 367bhp engine. This powers the raising and turning of the crane's boom.

STATS AND FACTS

FIRST BUILT: 2007

ORIGIN: GERMANY

POWER: 680BHP

LENGTH: 19.94M (65FT 5IN)

WIDTH: 3M (9FT 10IN)

HEIGHT: 4M (13FT 1IN)

WEIGHT: 94,000KG (207,235LB)

FUEL: DIESEL

Long, sturdy arms called outriggers extend out from the base of the truck to hold it firm and stable as the crane boom moves.

LTM 11200-9.1

O·9·1

LIEBHERR

DID YOU KNOW?

The eight sections of the boom slide out of each other when extending to a maximum height of 100m (328ft) – the height of some 25-floor buildings.

BIG RACING TRUCKS

It's not just monster trucks and tractors that pit their speed, power and agility against each other in races. Other sorts of trucks are raced for the adrenalin rush, the thrill of competition and to wow spectators.

PUT YOUR FOOT DOWN!

This sensational collection of racing trucks range from giant semis normally found hauling long, heavy trailers on roads, to lightning fast pickups and hefty rally racers that travel thousands of miles over tough terrain.

This shows the size of man compared to a big racing truck, in this case a Renault-MKR Technology Race truck.

BANKS FREIGHTLINER
PIKES PEAK RACER

This racer competes in the Pikes Peak International Hill Climb, a world famous hill climbing competition, and was built by 12-time Pikes Peak winner Mike Ryan. It's a giant truck which uses a Freightliner Cascadia as its base, and is usually seen hauling heavy loads on highways.

The Pikes Peak International Hill Climb is a tough test for both vehicle and driver as they hurtle round 156 turns and climb steeply, rising 1,440m (4,724ft) along the route covering 12.42 miles (19.99km), trying to record the fastest time.

STATS AND FACTS

FIRST BUILT: 2007

ORIGIN: US

FAMOUS DRIVERS: MIKE RYAN

POWER: APPROX. 2,400BHP

LENGTH: 6.1M (20FT)

HEIGHT: 2.79M (9FT 2IN)

WIDTH: 2.44M (8FT)

WEIGHT: 4,672KG (10,300LB)

FUEL: METHANOL

TRUCK STOP

Mike Ryan has worked as a stunt driver on over 500 TV shows and movies including *Terminator II, Herbie Fully Loaded* and *Fast and Furious 6.*

The truck's enormous Detroit DD60 14-litre engine weighs 1,197kg (2,640lb) and has twin turbochargers to generate huge power.

SUPER **BANKS** TURB

TOP

FREIGHTLINER

EVOLUTION FULLY SYNTHETIC DIESEL OIL

BRITISH PICKUP TRUCK RACER

An engine of 2–2.3 litres may sound small for truck racing, but when the vehicle they power weighs less than 900kg (2,000lb) the result is fast and furious action.

British Pickup Truck Racers accelerate rapidly and can reach speeds of over 140mph (225kph). Launched in 1997, the competition features two races per weekend over many laps of a racetrack with as many as 33 trucks taking part.

STATS AND FACTS

ORIGIN: UNITED KINGDOM

FIRST BUILT: 1997

MAXIMUM POWER: 229BHP

LENGTH: 4.2M (13FT 9 IN)

WIDTH: 1.79M (5FT 10IN)

HEIGHT: 3.34M (11FT)

WEIGHT: 870-885KG (1,918-1,951LB)

FUEL: SUPER UNLEADED PETROL

All teams use similar vehicles, so the racing can be very close, with lots of overtaking and trucks often just centimetres apart.

DID YOU KNOW?

Unlike many track-racing trucks, these pickups are kitted out with wet tyres and windscreen wipers to race in the rain.

CHEVROLET SILVERADO NASCAR TRUCK

NASCAR's Camping World Truck Series launched in 1995 and Silverado pickup trucks have taken part since 1999. They compete against pickups made by famous makes Dodge, Ford and Toyota in exciting track races which are held all over the United States and Canada.

A roll cage made of steel tubes protects the driver in his cab if the truck overturns.

TRUCK STOP

n average, over
,OOO fans attend
h of the 22 races
n the NASCAR
truck series
each year.

The Silverado's body is sleek and streamlined to cut through the air as it races at high speeds. In 2014 testing at the famous Daytona race track, Jeb Burton, driving a Silverado, reached a record speed of 191.144mph (307.6kph).

STATS AND FACTS

FIRST BUILT: 1998

ORIGIN: US

FAMOUS DRIVERS: AUSTIN DILLON, RON HORNADAY JR

POWER: 650–700BHP

LENGTH: 5.25M (17FT)

HEIGHT: 1.52M (5FT)

WIDTH: 2.03M (6FT 8IN)

WEIGHT: 1,542KG (3,400 LB) MINIMUM WITHOUT DRIVER BUT WITH FUEL

FUEL: 98 OCTANE E15 UNLEADED GASOLINE

KAMAZ 4326 DAKAR RALLY TRUCK

The Kamaz 4326 is a rugged vehicle built to tackle steep hills and sand dunes as well as race on more level ground at speeds of up to 102.5mph (165kph). Several fuel cells inside the truck body hold a total of 1,000 litres of fuel.

The powerful Yamz 8463. 10-07 engine is turbocharged and runs on diesel fuel.

The ultimate long-distance race, the Dakar Rally lasts more than two weeks and is run over 4,970–6,213 miles (8,000–10,000km) of tough terrain from muddy tracks to sandy deserts. Seventy hefty trucks took part in the 2014 rally in South America, but it was no surprise that a Kamaz truck was the winner. Kamaz trucks have won 10 of the previous 12 Dakar Rallies.

STATS AND FACTS

FIRST BUILT: 2003

ORIGIN: RUSSIA

FAMOUS DRIVERS: VLADIMIR CHAGIN, ANDREY KARGINOV

POWER: 850BHP

WEIGHT: 16,000KG (35,274LB) FULLY LOADED

LENGTH: APPROX. 7.7M (25FT)

HEIGHT: APPROX. 3.2M (10FT)

WIDTH: APPROX. 2.4M (8FT)

FUEL: DIESEL

DID YOU KNOW?

In 2010, Vladimir Chagin won the sixth of his record seven Dakar Rallies. He finished an hour ahead of another Kamaz truck and over 10 hours ahead of the third-placed truck!

MAN TGS RACE TRUCK

Big trucks like the MAN TGS are normally seen on the roads hauling heavy trailers, but they can be raced too. Competitions such as the FIA European Truck Championships pit more than 20 of these large trucks on the start line of racetracks.

A giant 12-litre turbo diesel engine gives the truck fast acceleration and high top speeds. In races, though, the truck's top speed is limited to 100mph (160kph).

TRUCK STOP

A MAN TGS can accelerate from 0–100mph (0–160kph) more quickly than a Porsche 911 sports car!

STATS AND FACTS

FIRST BUILT: 2008

ORIGIN: GERMANY

FAMOUS DRIVERS: JOCHEN HAHN, ANTONIO ALBACETE

MAXIMUM POWER: 1,100BHP

LENGTH: APPROX. 5.9M (19FT)

HEIGHT: APPROX. 2.8M (9FT)

WIDTH: APPROX. 2.5M (8FT)

WEIGHT: 5,500KG (12,125LB) MINIMUM WITH DRIVER BUT WITHOUT FUEL

FUEL: DIESEL OR BIO-DIESEL

Powerful multiple disc brakes are needed to slow these big rigs down on tight corners.

RENAULT-MKR TECHNOLOGY RACE TRUCK

Based in the Czech Republic village of Zidovice, the MKR team took Renault semi-trailer trucks and modified them to compete successfully in the European Truck Racing Championships.

Drivers need to work up and down the 16 gears of the truck's gearbox as they race.

In this championship, trucks race on some of Europe's most famous tracks including France's Le Mans and Germany's Nürburgring. With a powerful 12.8-litre racing engine and high-tech suspension, the Renault-MKR trucks proved fierce competitors. The trucks won both the 2010 and 2012 European Truck Racing Manufacturers' Championship crowns.

DID YOU KNOW?

As many as 120,000 spectators attend a typical European Truck Championship race weekend, which features four races.

STATS AND FACTS

FIRST BUILT: 2010

ORIGIN: CZECH REPUBLIC/FRANCE

FAMOUS DRIVERS: ADAM LACKO, MARKUS BÖSIGER

POWER: 1,160BHP

LENGTH: 5.6M (18FT)

WIDTH: 2.55M (8FT)

HEIGHT: 2.58M (8FT 5IN)

WEIGHT: 5,500KG (12,125LB) MINIMUM WITH DRIVER BUT WITHOUT FUEL

FUEL: DIESEL

SHOCKWAVE

Most big trucks and racing trucks are powered by land vehicle engines. Shockwave and Super Shockwave are trucks powered by jet engines normally found on military fighter jet aircraft making them the fastest trucks in the world.

Shockwave is powered by three jet engines. Each sucks in air, mixes it with fuel and sets the mixture alight. This generates hot gases which thrust out of the back of the engine, pushing the truck forward with massive power. It holds the world speed record for a big truck – 376mph (605kph).

Extra fuel injected into the hot gases behind the truck can produce spectacular flames more than 10m (33 ft) long.

STATS AND FACTS

FIRST BUILT: 1984

ORIGIN: US

FAMOUS DRIVERS: LES SHOCKLEY, CHRIS DARNELL

ENGINE: 3 PRATT & WHITNEY J34-48 JET ENGINES

POWER: 36,000BHP – 24 TIMES THE AMOUNT PRODUCED BY A TYPICAL MONSTER TRUCK ENGINE

WEIGHT: 3,084KG (6,800LB)

LENGTH: 8.5M (28FT)

FUEL: AVIATION FUEL

TRUCK STOP

Shockwave sometimes races aircraft at shows. It uses parachutes along with its wheel brakes to slow down.

TATA PRIMA
RACE TRUCK 4038.S

A brand new truck-racing competition was unveiled in 2014 – the T1 Prima Truck Racing Championship. Twelve Prima 4038.S trucks, built by Tata Daewoo, compete on six different racetracks throughout India.

Strong netting over the windows keeps the driver's arms and head inside the cab.

DID YOU KNOW?

A regular Tata Prima 4038.S ready to drive on roads can weigh up to 18,000kg (39,683lb) fully loaded.

Each truck has been modified for racing, including upgrades to the brakes and a racing harness to hold the driver safely in place in all situations. The trucks race along at speeds of up to 68mph (110kph).

STATS AND FACTS

FIRST BUILT: 2008

ORIGIN: INDIA/SOUTH KOREA

FAMOUS DRIVERS: STEVE HORNE, TWO-TIME WINNER OF THE BRITISH TRUCK RACING CHAMPIONSHIPS

POWER: 370BHP

WEIGHT: 5,000-6,000KG EMPTY (11,023-13,227LB)

LENGTH: 6.13M (20FT)

HEIGHT: 3.32M (10FT 10IN)

WIDTH: 2.58M (8FT 5IN)

FUEL: DIESEL

TOYOTA TUNDRA NASCAR TRUCK

In 2004, Toyota became the first new pickup truck manufacturer in decades to enter NASCAR competitions, with their Toyota Tundra vehicle. It's been a huge success, winning five titles.

DID YOU KNOW?

In 2013, 17-year-old Erik Jones, driving a Toyota Tundra, became the youngest ever winner of a NASCAR truck race, the Lucas Oil 150 in Phoenix, Arizona.

Like all trucks in the NASCAR Camping World Truck Series, the Tundra has a 68-litre (18-gallon) fuel tank. During long races, trucks head into the pits to refuel. Some races cover distances of over 250m (400km).

A spoiler is the large wing on the back of the truck which forces air downwards. It helps the truck grip the track at high speeds.

STATS AND FACTS

FIRST BUILT: 2004

ORIGIN: US/JAPAN

FAMOUS DRIVERS: MATT CRAFTON, TODD BODINE, ERIK JONES

POWER: 650BHP

LENGTH: 5.25M (17FT)

HEIGHT: 1.52M (5FT)

WIDTH: 2.03M (6FT 8IN)

WEIGHT: 1,542KG (3,400 LB) MINIMUM WITHOUT DRIVER BUT WITH FUEL

FUEL: 98 OCTANE E15 UNLEADED GASOLINE

V8 UTE RACING SERIES

The ute, short for utility vehicle, is a type of high-performance pickup truck that's very popular in Australia. This race series pits the two biggest ute makers against each other as 16 Holden SS utes compete against an equal number of Ford Falcon XR8s.

With all the utes closely matched in power and performance, racing (three races per weekend) is often tight and tough. Many side panels are dented and wing mirrors knocked off as the vehicles try to squeeze past each other on the track.

Each car carries a live action video camera inside. The camera's footage can be used to judge if a driver is at fault when a crash occurs.

STATS AND FACTS

ORIGIN: AUSTRALIA/US

POWER: 350-400BHP

LENGTH: APPROX. 4.9M (16FT)

WIDTH: APPROX. 1.9M (6FT 2IN)

HEIGHT: APPROX. 1.5M (5FT)

WEIGHT: 1,800 OR 1,850KG (3,968LB OR 4,078LB)

FUEL: HIGH OCTANE GASOLINE RACING FUEL

TRUCK STOP

V8 Ute racing driver Cam Wilson also holds the world record for the longest distance raced in a go-kart in 24 hours – a staggering 375 miles (604km) or 3,554 laps of a track.

RECORD BREAKERS

FAST AND FURIOUS

For many years, Bigfoot 14 was the fastest known monster truck with a top speed of 69mph (111kph). That was shattered in 2011 by Kirk Dabney in Maximum Overkill, which roared to a top speed of 90.44mph (145.5kph).

TALL AND MIGHTY

Bigfoot 5 is the tallest and heaviest ever monster truck. Standing on its gigantic 3.05m (10ft) tyres, the truck weighs a hefty 12.7 tonnes (28,000lb).

Each of Bigfoot 5's enormous tyres weighs around 1,088kg (2,400lb).

THE LONG ROAD

Road trains feature two or more trailers pulled by a single truck. The longest ever road train, in 2006, featured a Mack truck pulling an astonishing 112 trailers behind it. The truck and trailers measured 1,473.3m (4,837ft).

DID YOU KNOW?

In 1999 Bigfoot 14 managed to jump over a Boeing 727 airliner. The record leap was measured at 62m (202ft)!

PICKING UP SPEED

The Banks Sidewinder Dakota is the fastest ever diesel-fuelled pickup truck with a top speed of 222.1mph (357kph).

GLOSSARY

ACCELERATION The act of making a truck or another vehicle speed up and go faster.

AIRBRUSH A tool which uses compressed air to blow paint through a nozzle.

ALUMINIUM A metal used for some truck parts that can be light in weight but very strong.

BATTERY A store of chemicals in a case which, when connected to a circuit, supplies electricity.

BED The floor or bottom of a truck where cargo can be stored.

BHP Brake horsepower, a measure of an engine's power output.

BIG RIG Nickname for large semi-trailer trucks made of a powered truck and one or more detachable trailers.

BODY Main part of a vehicle, which houses the driver, passengers and/or cargo.

BONNET A body panel, usually made of metal, which can open to reveal the truck's engine. Also known as a hood.

BRAKES Parts of a vehicle which slow it down.

BULL BARS A device mounted on the front of a vehicle to protect the driver and passengers in case of a collision with a large animal.

CAB The part of the truck where the driver sits, steers and controls the vehicle.

CHASSIS The frame of a truck that supports the vehicle and key parts like the engine and bodywork.

CO-DRIVER A person who shares the driving of a racing vehicle.

CRANE BOOM The long strut or pole which can lift loads up and down in the air.

CRASH TENDER A specially built fire truck mostly used at airports, designed to travel fast and carry fire-fighting chemicals and water.

DIESEL A type of fuel made from oil, used in many truck engines.

DISC BRAKES A type of brake where pads press against a turning disc to slow the wheel down.

DUMP TRUCK A type of truck which carries rock, earth or other loose materials and can tip them out of their large container.

ENGINE The part of the truck which generates the power to move it forward.

EXHAUST Tubes which carry waste gases away from a truck's engine.

FIBREGLASS A strong, light material made of plastic reinforced by fibres of glass running through it.

FOUR-WHEEL DRIVE A truck that has power delivered to all four of its wheels.

FUEL A substance that is burned to produce heat or power, such as diesel or methanol.

GEARS System in a truck which helps a truck change speed without damaging the engine.

HOPPER The name given to the large container on a dump truck that holds rock, earth, coal or other loose materials.

HYBRID TRUCKS Vehicles which have both a petrol engine and an electric motor or motors.

HYDRAULIC PISTON A rod that is moved up and down a cylinder by liquids in the cylinder.

LEXAN A strong, shatterproof polycarbonate resin often used for windows and windscreens.

MECHANIC Someone who can fix and repair motor vehicles.

MONSTER JAM A tour and competition run by Feld Entertainment for many of North America's leading monster trucks.

NASCAR The National Association for Stock Car Auto Racing, a type of car and truck racing competition on tracks in North America.

OFF-ROAD To travel in a vehicle away from roads and on tracks, trails or open ground.

OPEN PIT MINE A mine where coal or metals in rocks are retrieved from a giant hole dug in the ground.

OUTRIGGERS Posts or struts which extend out from a crane truck's body to keep the truck stable.

PICKUP TRUCK A small truck with an open flat cargo area behind the driver's cab.

PITS An area close to a race track where vehicles can leave the track to receive new tyres, to refuel or for their team to make repairs.

PUMP A machine that raises or lifts a liquid or gas.

RACING HARNESS A type of secure seat belt attached to the seat frame which keeps a racing driver securely in place should there be a crash or accident.

ROAD TRAIN A powerful truck hauling two, three or more trailers full of cargo.

ROLL CAGE A frame, often made of steel tubes, which protects a driver should their vehicle crash and overturn.

SPOILER A panel or wing fitted to a racing truck that directs air to keep the truck gripping the ground.

STEEL A strong metal alloy usually made by combining iron with carbon.

STREAMLINED A truck or body part shaped so that air flows easily over and around it.

SUSPENSION Springs and shock absorbers attached to a vehicle's wheels which help ensure a smoother ride when travelling over bumpy surfaces.

SUV Sports utility vehicle, a large estate car that usually has four-wheel drive so that it can travel off-road.

TAILGATE The hinged flap at the back of a pickup truck which can open or close.

TANK A large container used to store fuel in a truck.

TERRA TYRES Giant tyres with a chunky outer surface which grips muddy ground well. These were originally found on large farm vehicles.

THRUST A pushing force created in a jet engine that helps propel a jet engine-powered vehicle forward.

TONNE A unit of measurement equal to 1,000kg.

TRAILER The wheeled container holding cargo that a large truck pulls.

TYRE A ring-shaped covering, usually made of rubber, which encloses a wheel and is the part of a truck that is in contact with the ground.

UTE Short for utility vehicle, a type of pickup truck popular in Australia.

WHEELBASE The distance between the middle of the front and back wheels of a vehicle.

WHEEL TETHERS Strong steel cables keep the wheels tied to the truck in case of a crash.

WHEELIE Lifting the front wheels of a monster truck off the ground and driving only on the rear wheels.

PICTURE CREDITS